Letter to the Prime Minister

Justus Siage

Nsemia

Author: Justus Siage
Cover Design: Danielle Pitt
Cover Design Concept: Justus Siage
Design and Layout: Kemunto Matunda

Note to Librarians:
A Cataloguing record for this book is available from the
Library and Archives Canada.

ISBN: 978-1-926906-08-9

First Published July 2011
Published By: **Nsemia Inc. Publishers; www.nsemia.com**

DEDICATION

This book is dedicated to my two adorable sisters and only siblings: Winnie and Grace.
Something I have never told them before: they have been a great inspiration to me in both my writing and other undertakings of life. I love them very much; I am sure they will be proud of me through this work.

FOREWORD

As James A. Michener once said, *'If a man happens to find himself, he has a mansion which he can inhabit with dignity all the days of his life.'* In writing, Justus has found his purpose: to share knowledge and wisdom through art.

Letter to The Prime Minister glides the reader through the typical, day to day situations that ordinary Kenyans find themselves in. Justus is a young writer who expresses his frustration with the current economic, social and political standings of the country. He entwines both blunt and humorous language to put his point across.

The book is divided into small sections that take the reader through a journey of the author's personal experiences and the happenings affecting the country's development. This is his attempt to communicate to the government of the day what the young aspire for tomorrow. He also addresses the citizen, to spur the local person to positive behaviour and action.

Some of the issues that he touches on include the Kenyan Constitution, unrest in boarding schools, traffic jams, and high cost of living, amongst many other ills in Kenyan society. These are presented in the form of a letter to the country's Prime Minister. He hopes that the PM will respond to his 'letter' and make the necessary changes for the sake of the country.

Kenya is an intriguing country. The myriad of issues faced by the citizen are sure to overwhelm one who takes on the task of narrating to an outsider. Justus has done this brilliantly by using witty language, one that appeals to both the young and old.

Justus is a college student who has not allowed his age to stand in his way of doing what he enjoys doing – writing. He has written other artistic pieces before, which are educative and inspirational. He uses almost the same style to drive his points through. On reading this book, I see a Justus who yearns to make a difference in the society, a Justus who wishes that leaders could stop thinking about themselves and instead work for the masses – a calling that they vowed to safeguard.

Just like in his first published book *Billionaire Dropout* Justus succeeds in entertaining, educating, challenging and inspiring readers with his creative style. He does not shy away from directing very sensitive questions to one of the most powerful people in government. He shares his divergent views on issues that have been informed or determined by the 'majority' wave. He is not afraid of taking a controversial stand, so long as he backs it with an ingenious theory which he shares in this book. For example, he believes that the country needs to take care of more urgent problems like hunger, unemployment and corruption before spending so much money on a new Constitution. You need to read the section to embrace where he is coming from. In the end, everything that he writes makes sense.

I have had the privilege of reading the book more than once. The first time I got the manuscript, I dismissed it for I assumed that a young man who had yet to complete college could not write anything 'book worthy'. When I finally decided to read it, I was captivated from the beginning to the end.... I found it quite relevant and did not want to put it down. It is interesting and when you read, you feel like you are having a conversation with the author about the issues raised. The reader will easily connect with every part of *Letter to The Prime Minister*.

Beatrice Adera Amollo
Head Librarian,
Australian Studies Institute (AUSI)

ABOUT THE AUTHOR

Justus Siage is the second born in a family of three children, sandwiched between two adorable ladies – Winnie and Grace.

He sat for his KCPE in 2006 after which he joined high school, which he completed in 2010 having sat for his IGCSE O-levels. He is currently pursuing undergraduate studies in International Business at the Australian Studies Institute (AUSI) in Nairobi.

Justus has a deep interest in the business world and economic issues in particular. He is constantly in search of solutions and the way forward for many of the economic, social, environmental and political problems that Kenya faces. Justus aims at improving Kenyans' living conditions, and making life a little more pleasant for the average Kenyan.

In many ways, he is an average Kenyan teenager in jeans. However, unlike the average jeans-wearing teen, Justus began writing at an early age, publishing his first book, *Billionaire Dropout* (Sahel Books Inc. 2009) at the age of 17.

ACKNOWLEDGEMENTS

This book has been a special journey that has involved many people, with some of them taking part in it unknowingly.

Three years ago, my uncle – Dan Siage – saw me through a life-changing experience that enabled me to discover my writing abilities. Thanks to him, I have been able to write this book.

I would also like to thank my uncle, Jeremiah Siage, who has been of great help throughout the whole process of putting the book together and getting it ready for publication.

Beatrice Adera Amollo, the Head Librarian at my college, was kind enough to go out of her way to read through my work and give me feedback. She has been very helpful and supportive of me.

My mum, dad, sisters and friend –Roy – have also all been very supportive and at times they have unknowingly helped me put the book together.

A big thank you goes out to all of them!

Letter to the Prime Minister

Have you ever felt the irritation of someone arguing with you over the spelling of your middle name as if they know it better than you do?

That's the kind of irritation I've been feeling these past few weeks after some amateur dared to drag me into an argument over the Hummer H2. How dare she (an illiterate in the car-world) dispute me, a petrol-head of all people, on such an issue?

If the topic of discussion happened to be women's hair or something like that, I would have been least concerned by her rubbishing of my every word. But when it comes to cars, someone without the slightest knowledge of what to do next after placing a key in a vehicle's ignition should definitely be the last person to dare spark an argument with me on such a subject.

Damn!

It's been long since anything went this deep under my skin. I just had to let it out to someone. And who would be better placed than yourself (a man who actually owns a H2) to hear me out? No other name comes to mind, which is the very reason I'm sharing this ordeal of mine with you.

Boy, hasn't she pissed me off! She grew up here in Kenya but now happens to work somewhere in the Middle Eastern desert, some place known as Dubai. And as we all know, that area is damn rich thanks to its controlling power of the global-oil-market, and the business hub it has become these past few years. That means that some individuals there are able to keep the people's eyes well-fed on the dashing beauty of the goddesses of the motor world. This young lady happens to form part of the crowd that binges on this yummy eye-candy.

Because of all this free intemperate feasting, her eyes have deluded her mind into believing she actually knows about cars.

Oops! Sorry... I've not explained to you how this bitter argument sparked off. Have I? I think I should do that right away, before I go any further. Excuse the hiccup.

It all began when a-lack-of-anything-better-to-do on a weekday evening made me join this young lady (whom I'll call T) in watching a local program on telly of which, ironically, I'm not the slightest fan. I was so bored and my mind wasn't being of much help either. It just sat there and completely refused to think up a more interesting way of killing time. So I sat there on the sofa, too, bored out of my paralyzed mind and nearly falling asleep when lo! and behold something worth beholding popped up on the screen. For a moment, the TV appeared to come to life and smack the drowsiness out of my eyes, making me sit up straight again. For a second, I feared this was nothing but the vile creation of my untamed mind that was now very high on boredom.

Luckily for me, this was no mirage, it was real! We all saw her (the lady on the screen) in her dashing beauty – the Hummer H2; a black one in fact. Very quickly, without much thought, T, who was sitting next to me, dissed[i] the car, called it fake and went ahead to mention that there were better Hummers "where she's from". Can you imagine that?

I'm neither a petty person, nor am I overly unreasonable. Therefore, I was kind enough to engage the services of the organ that does all my thinking for me to rationalize and analyze fully the deeper meaning of her words before deciding on what to do next.

The conclusion?

i   *Informal for dismissed*

Her motive was either to indirectly floss[ii] to me how superior stuff in Dubai are ("where she is from") to here, or she was just being a bitter old hater! The latter being what I settled for.

That was it for me! I couldn't just sit there and take such an insult! You know, I've been seriously considering taking her to court with charges of uttering a hate speech. The only thing still barring me is that I'm not sure I have enough patience to walk the slow path of justice. It'd probably be years, if not decades, before the case is heard and justice served.

A quicker remedy could be sought from Clarkson (the dude from Top Gear). I've actually considered talking to him as well about it, but I'm afraid he might overreact and go ahead to literally carry out some of the extremely silly acts of vengeance that I only dare go to the extent of thinking about. So to avoid taking a bigger bite than my mouth can possibly hold, I think I'll leave him out of this.

You, as a man who actually owns one of these American war machines, do you know of anything in the range that's superior in any tiny way to the H2?

Because last I checked, the H1 was great for only two kinds of people:

1. Ex-service men who want to re-live their Iraqi experience in the comfort of their home towns.
2. Non-service men who are too chicken to go to Iraq but still want to have the experience of riding in a combat vehicle.

For anyone who falls in any of these two categories, this is the car to buy. It's huge, it's ugly, it's set-up for a battle field (except for the guns and arsenal), and it will therefore quickly find a soft spot in your heart.

However, if you are a bit more civilized and just want vulgarity, the H2 is your solution. It's still big, but unlike the H1, it's got a little sense of look. I mean,

ii   *Informal for 'show off'*

getting your girlfriend (or wife, in your case) to join you on a ride in it isn't such a hassle. That's good!

And its little snot-nosed sister, the H3, is the car for someone who's always wanted a Hummer but both his wallet and garage aren't large enough to accommodate one. The guys at General Motors custom-made this thing for this very individual. In my world, in one word, I'd call it USELESS! Honestly, I'd much rather buy a Jeep or a pair of sneakers and walk to my destination.

In simple English, the H2 is definitely the coolest amongst these three cars. So other than the ones I've talked about, please do inform me if you know of any other mass-market Hummer that's currently available, that's cooler than the H2. Mark my words "currently available". Forget the concept cars and all, just look at what's out there already.

Do you see anything better than the H2? I bet you, there's none!

Dress her up in twenty six-inch chrome with a splash of cologne, tint and make-up, and she's good to appeal to any woman, especially if she is French or Italian. So for anyone to dare rubbish the H2 is a clear indication of their illiteracy in the motor-world. I sure did well not to continue with the argument and let it die out, for it would have not made me look any brighter than her.

That aside, let me get down to writing your letter before you start questioning my level of education given that I seem to have defied the English teacher's basic laws of letter writing. But I assure you, there's no cause for alarm. I just had to first let out this thing that has been bugging me. So here you go with your letter.

February, 2011

Dear Mr. Prime Minister,

How is the going? I guess you are doing fine. Are you as proud as Alfred Mutua to be Kenyan?

I'm not sure if I'm the only one who seems to notice, but time has really picked up the pace lately. Honestly, the rate at which it drew the curtain on 2010 is on an all new level! I can't believe another year is gone by already and that we are now in 2011. That was quick! Too quick in fact. It's almost like a joke!

On the last day of 2010, I kept asking myself, "For real, is this the very last evening of 2010?" I couldn't believe it!

I spent that day traveling back to Nairobi from Kisumu. Such trips aren't anything to write home, let alone anywhere, about. However, this particular one may be a bit different. It may actually be a story worth telling.

To start with, allow me to point out that there's never been a way for the budget-traveler, like myself, to enjoy a Kisumu-Nairobi flight. Until now that is...

As it turns out, there's a new airline that offers Nairobi-Kisumu flights for the same rate as a bus. Not bad, huh? In case you are a fan of numbers, I'll inform you that the flight takes six hours, thanks to the fact that the plane flies low (on the road).

It's pretty awesome! The seats are comfy. It has an internal pit-latrine, two TVs, air-con, two sun-roofs, footrests that are like tractor clutch pedals. And last but not least, each seat has an overhead lamp that I believe is intended to aid night-travelers to pick up their chips that drop as they feast aboard.

I'm also sure it has a fabulous engine because of

what the man who drives it told me, together with my understanding of a vehicle wearing the Scania badge. It makes a wonderful noise too during gear change; you'd not want the driver to quit shifting! You'd think it has a tuned exhaust or something.

For the undiscerning eye, it may be all perfect like a marriage made in the world of magic and fantasy. Unfortunately, I don't have such an eye. Mine are designed to see things as they are in this world we call reality. Therefore when I now think of it, I'm convinced it would have been a much better use of money to just board a normal bus. Coz when I weigh the ups against the downs of this thing, it's being priced the same as a normal bus is too expensive.

Here is why: first of all, there is the sickening name that you'd rather not tell your friends about as it'd only make you their laughing stock. I mean, how many people go through the list of possible names for PSVs[i] in this world and settle for *The Guardian*? If you ask me, the guy who had the role of picking out a name for this vehicle did a whack job! For a security firm or a dog it would be a superb name... but for a vehicle that carries passengers? I'm sorry, but I don't think there can possibly be a worse pick than this!

Secondly, there is the suspension made from what I believe is chicken wire. It's far too wobbly and willowy. When it hits a bump, the vehicle dances wildly as though it were performing at some silly concert.

My idle staring at things also served to constantly point out to me that this must be a *mtumba*[ii] vehicle from some bus company in Europe. But other than what my mind kept telling me, I really have no concrete evidence to support the notion, other than

---

i   *Public Service Vehicles*

ii   *Kiswahili for second hand*

the folded polythene on the TV screens and the rusty look of some grill that was over the seat I called mine.

I think it would be wise for me to stop there. Anything else I point out about this vehicle at this point will either be unnecessary whining or horn-blowing. I don't want to bore you with either. Let me just say if you want to have a long Kisumu-Nairobi flight using the highway without spending much money, there's now a way of doing so.

Back to time: I wasn't done talking about this 2010-2011 transition, was I?

My 2010 started off on a great note. I doubt if it could really get much better than that. You see, in my world, for a year to begin with the launch of a darling such as the Range Rover Sport 2010 would only be second to having it actually parked in his driveway, in making a boy's heart leap with joy. What a thrill that was for both the men who bought it and those who downloaded its pictures to use as desktop backgrounds on their personal computers. (This is one of those few things that's appreciated by both those who possess it and those who don't. It's a bit like football – loved and strongly debated upon by those who can play and those who can't.)

So that was the launch of my 2010! But fate didn't have smooth sailing in store for me. My year that had started perfectly suffered a serious anticlimax from sometime in late December, Christmas to be exact. And this low mood ushered in my 2011.

I may be alone on this, but I don't get what the big fuss is about Christmas. Really, in this corner of the globe what more is to it other than intemperate feasting and drinking? All we do is travel up country or someplace else to indulge in food and drink like there is no tomorrow. There is absolutely no value added to life, other than a few extra kilos. What vanity!

And the saddest bit to me is the vast majority of us don't seem to remember that Boxing Day comes right after Christmas and that it's a time for us to share our abundance with the less fortunate. Instead of giving out the food to those who need it, we let it sit in our fridges until it is fit for only the bin!

But that's always been a bugging issue to me; I can't claim it just came up this particular December. So clearly something else sprang up and added to my disappointment this particular Christmas. I'm saddened to admit that my personal issues may be the ones to blame. I guess the bitter disappointment I suffered was just too much to ignore.

It all began when Christmas night presented me with a very rare opportunity, one of those chances that don't knock on your door too often. Therefore as expected, I took it gladly with all the joy the little boy in me could possibly muster. I knew this was going to be fun, I knew it would be one of the most thrilling things I had done all year. So when opportunity presented itself, there was no way on earth I was going to turn it down!

It was the chance to drive the flagship of one of Germany's most reputed car makers – the Mercedes Benz S-class. And the best part of the deal, for me, was that it wasn't from my pocket! It wasn't going to cost me a coin! I jumped in and plumped myself on the driver's enormous sofa, which reminded me of what it felt like to try on Dad's coats when I was 10. Without letting this feeling of puniness dampen my spirit, I fastened my seat belt, adjusted the seat and set off on what I hoped would be one of the most thrilling drives that year.

Without mincing words, let me say of the drive that it was very dull for me. I appreciate the concept of luxury and comfort but what was portrayed by this car is an exaggeration. When you add up the figures and do your math right, all looks very good. In simpler terms this car is unbelievable on paper, and one would expect nothing less of a monster on the road!

But when you get out of your calculator and go onto the real roads, all you see is a harmless creature that only eats up the miles pretty fast!

Honestly, it's quick! Really quick! Again (if you like figures) let me say of the engine: the Mercedes 3.2 litre V6 under the hood sure pumps out a lot of power that propels the car's enormous weight as fast as your right foot would like it to go. So as far as speed and power are concerned, it's the real deal. There is a problem however, and that is only the speedometer and rushing scenery serves to confirm how fast you are actually going. Everything else is just calm and quiet like nothing is happening. It offers absolutely no thrill of speed! It's like a plane – moves quickly but passengers hardly notice or feel the rush. That kind of spoils it for me coz I'd like my heartbeat to move in tune with the speedometer. I want to feel its beat rise as rapidly as the speedometer pin on the dashboard.

I'd say this car gave me a Christmas present, in fact the only present I received. Its present was a message neatly wrapped in boredom that said: This is a grown up car for grown-ups only! There's no room for boys like you who still want thrill!

I found that to be a bit of a stab in the back given all the high esteem in which I held that car. I was also a bit tormented because knowing that is Mercedes' business class vehicle, it could as well be what my future has in store for me given that my career ambitions lie in the corporate world. Such unmatched levels of dullness would require quite a lot of getting used to on my part.

So that was my Christmas! And the pace-setter for the ushering in of my 2011! Not fun at all I must say! And the extremely hot and dry weather wasn't of much help either.

On a brighter note, this period of winding up 2010 and ushering in the New Year has provided me time to relax and recollect as I strategize for the year ahead. A personal commitment I've made to myself is to ensure this year is different. So I guess I have to do the necessary planning and put measures in place to ensure my goals are actualized. Otherwise it will just be disaster!

This is serious. It's not just some New Year resolution that will soon be forgotten and never followed through. Let me put it like this: I've made a contract with the tenant of my head that this year he's going to have to pay up for all I've been doing for him. I'm talking big... it's not peanuts I'm after. I want something big from him! You know what I mean?

I'm not sure you have been as privileged as myself, with ample time to recollect and plot for the New Year, but you must still have a plate-full, given all the uncertainties that have been terrorizing the world of politics lately.

Anyway, I hope the family's good? I saw you went home for Christmas.

Our First Lady together with your lady (I don't know the title to give her) have both kept very low profiles lately. How come? Is this some sort of pact they made or something? Hope she (your lady) is okay though. Remind her that we need to be seeing a bit more of her in the public limelight. Pass her my warm regards.

Say hi to everyone else I may be bothered enough to know, too.

I ain't doing too bad myself. I had a little irritation

on my teeth a short while back, which forced me to pay the tooth doctor a visit for the first time since... never, I believe. I can't recall ever having to visit the dentist over my own teeth. I've always hated the hospital (especially the dentist's) for no tangible reason, until now that is.

The tooth doctor sure gave me a reason to hate the damn place! A wuss I'm not, that's for sure. But I don't voluntarily subject my body to unnecessary pain. It's just being human, you know, being a normal decent creature with something of value between the ears.

So being this normal decent thing that I am, the first thing I asked this man and his assistant was "will this hurt?"

"Why are you asking us when you are already in pain?" That's the trash-talk the dude had to throw back at me!

What the hell? Who told them I was in pain? I certainly didn't and neither did I have pain written all over my face. I had an irritation partially from my back teeth that had a slight problem, and from Mum constantly bugging me to go get them cleaned. I didn't have any pain whatsoever from my teeth!

If in any case this guy was reading what was written on my face, he would have seen a big "This won't end well if you carry on like that, Mr.!" I had sat in the waiting room for ages (the doctors had a meeting) and this was the last thing I needed.

Why was this guy bringing for me? It's not like I'm the one who told him to be a dentist. The fact that he wakes up every morning to come and shove his head down people's mouths for a living has nothing to do with me!

But I kept my cool. I was taught not to mess with those under whose mercy I still am, lest they decide to get even. Know what I mean?

The assistant gave me some bits of cardboard to bite on as he x-rayed my teeth. The dentist had vanished again at this point. He probably went for another meeting, who knows!

I wonder what they discuss. Coz in just about every hospital I've been to, there's a time in the day when the healers disappear into a room for a meeting.

"Too many people are getting well too quick."

"Our ICU[iii] is empty; we need to fill it up urgently!"

Or "Too many people are not dying in this facility." Are these the sort of issues they talk about? Coz what else would be so important as to deserve a meeting every other hour?

Let me not jump to conclusions. But whatever it is they talk about in those meetings, they need to find a better time and place for them! If you were really sick by the time you got to hospital, you could die in the queue just waiting to get in to see the doctor!

Anyway, the x-ray wasn't a problem, no pain on my part! I tried hard to clip the assistant's fingers between my sharp shark-like teeth. Unfortunately, I failed! But apart from that setback, the x-ray went well.

When the films were finally developed, the dentist reappeared from god knows where. For about forever and 30 minutes, three men sat there staring at photos of crooked teeth. One of the men (the specialist) was constantly adjusting his glasses and craning his head closer to the images, probably to get a better view.

My short span of concentration on such boring stuff soon wore out and my big mouth blubbered out "what does it show?"

I've not yet fully understood why, but my question was quickly watered down with big terms picked up in the hallways of med-school, before the weapons

---

iii   *Intensive Care Unit*

were picked up and horror generously dished out to my poor teeth.

For the first time in my life, the dental weapons of torture were pointed at me! The creepy sounds of grinding teeth that I'd merely listened to from the lobby whenever I brought other casualties to this place were now to be created from my few crooked teeth. This time I was the guinea pig on the operating table... not too fun a place to be, I'll tell you that.

You know the way peoples' lives drastically change after a near death experience and stuff? I think I underwent a similar transition, only more severe. I now brush my teeth twice a day, no sweat! I'm even considering reducing my intake of sweet tooth-poisons.

That's just how creepy what I went through was! Even those who come back from the grave don't change so drastically.

———

By the way, for a few months now, I've been one of your constituents. Not by voter-registration, but by geographical placing. Yes, I now live in Langata.

From what I've seen so far, I can say it's a specimen of the greater Kenya with all the paradoxes and ironies of this nation of ours. I doubt that reaching out to your wide scope of voters is anything close to being called a piece of cake. In order to appeal to the rich, the middle class, and even the poor who live in shanty *mabati*[iv] structures to all unite in voting you into office is definitely an uphill task. That really is some work.

As far as I'm concerned, I don't have much to talk about in regards to Langata. I'd say it is an okay place (the part where I live). Apart from the traffic at

---

iv   *Iron sheet*

certain times of the day on Langata Road, and the old bombs that serve as *matatus*[v] in this end of town, I'm comfortable enough.

But I guess I can't single out Langata when it come to slow traffic, as this is pretty much part and parcel of life in this city. I guess it is part of "The Nairobi Dream" (if such a thing exists).

Honestly, I like Nairobi. I don't mind the chilly weather at certain times of the year, I don't mind its big size, and I certainly don't mind all the fun places to go. Without mincing my words, I can say of it: it's a nice place.

However, I'd have to be a bigger liar than a fisherman who talks of a tiny fish he caught as though it were a whale, to tell you I don't mind the traffic. Gosh! It drives me insane! Within these few months that I've lived here, I've already lost count of all the hours of my life that have been wasted sitting in traffic.

One morning I spent more than an hour on Langata Road! The traffic wasn't moving, for ages it was ground to a halt. I felt like getting out of the car and continuing my journey on foot, which would have added a bit more mileage on my shoes but would have obviously been much quicker.

What I fail to understand is this: how come cops are the ones controlling traffic at roundabouts that have functional lights? I mean, why spend so much money fitting those lights if they don't serve their purpose? This must definitely be one of the main contributors to slow traffic.

Those lights are (or at least should be) programmed to ensure the traffic is properly regulated at all junctions and roundabouts so that it flows smoothly. There's absolutely no way a bunch of cops can pull

---

v   *Small public service vehicles (PSVs) in Kenya.*

off the kind of coordination that these lights can.

An observation I've made is that we (Kenyans) tend to follow rules best when there's someone of authority standing next to us ready to breathe fire down our backs when we get out of line. Therefore we usually put our minds on idle and jump lights when there's no cop to watch over us. So maybe that's why those boys (and an occasional girl) in uniform have been permanently deployed to our roundabouts.

The problem is therefore not the lights. It is us not being able to follow rules without surveillance. So the cops should be deployed not to control traffic, but to baby-sit us and spank the bad kids who get out of line! That way the lights will be able to do their work properly and our traffic nightmare will be contained. Simple as such!

There's really no need for us to continue burning so much time and fuel in unnecessary traffic jams. I wish I could get through to the guys who are in charge of the traffic in this city and have a chat on the way forward. I may not know too much about city planning, but I sure have lots of tricks under my sleeves that may prove helpful.

And this traffic menace doesn't end with the many cars on the roads, does it?

As it turns out, when you get to town and step out of your car and onto the streets, you find nothing but another jam – one made up of people. The streets are ever congested, especially during the morning rush and in the evening when everyone is making their way back to their dwelling places. It is so frustrating to walk in the city at such peak hours as everyone keeps bumping into you.

Before moving to Nairobi, I was initially in the lake side city of Kisumu. I've lived there for ages and this change of environment was truly deserved. When I finally left that place and became your constituent, I thought I'd said goodbye to the two things that form the back-bone of life in that city: persistent blackouts and dry taps.

Honestly, in Kisumu persistent blackouts are a freaky thing that residents must learn to live with!

No, wait a minute. I don't mean freaky, do I? I mean annoying, irritating, something that is a gigantic pain in one of those wrong places.

Are we communicating?

In case I'm not making sense to you, allow me to put it like this: there are some things that, over time, people learn to stomach and somehow live with. But there are those that can't share a similar fate!

For example, when a star who's got it made decides to sing something to brag and diss everyone else (their fans included), no one really makes a fuss. We accept the peculiar individual and even listen to the song for a while, even though we know very well we are the ones being dissed.

But when some other lunatic who's always been, still is, and will always be a loser, decides to sing about how fly she/he is, we call them a "wannabe" and diss them and the trash they sing!

This is what street law declares, and the principle behind this law applies to virtually everything else that anyone who's capable of thought may ever comprehend.

That means KPLC[vi] is no exception! In Kisumu when lights go coz it's about to rain, no one complains.

---

vi   *Kenya Power and Lighting Company*

Even the few who use solar and other alternative sources of electricity turn them off and join everyone else in darkness. The folk have all somehow accepted and found a way to live with the fact that electricity in that part of the world is scared of rain (much like the people)!

However, when the sun is up like it usually is most parts of the year and lights still go out for prolonged periods (like whole days), we have reason to ask why and even get pissed about it.

This is utter absurdity by the company! I always thought there was something not quite right with the management of KPLC's Kisumu branch. But to my disappointment, this ludicrousness isn't limited to the Kisumu branch only, and if in any case it were, then it must have followed me to your constituency. I mean, a short while back, we were having blackouts in Langata at times when no reason was really eminent for such interruptions.

I don't know if it's in your power to do something about it. But you must have a few strings you can pull to straighten stuff out. Please pull them, or even better, hook me up so that I do the pulling! I am ready to pay the political price for that.

But still, what do you have to lose? I mean, if you sorted that out, the people using KPLC services would all vote in your favor come 2012. And that's not a small crowd!

You've got to hear this; a friend of mine posted it on their wall on Facebook during the company's rights issue: *KPLC should focus on the 'lights issue' rather than the 'rights issue'.*

How more on point could one possibly put this, huh? This is truly a bombshell!

Anyway, despite my disappointment with the

stima[vii] boys of Langata, so far I've found a bit of consolation from the *maji*[viii] boys. But I think luck has had a lot to do with it, coz my friends who live in a neighbouring estate don't seem to be as pleased with these *maji* boys, thanks to their dry taps most of the time. Tough luck for them, I must say!

I'm not sure if their *maji* boys deserve the same penalty, but those who supply residents of Kisumu with water (they call themselves KIWASCO[ix]) should perhaps be drowned! They provide some of the lousiest services one can ever imagine! The worst part is people are paying for it! It's a shameful paradox to live on the shores of a massive fresh water lake and still suffer dry taps.

Not that I've ever had them mention it, but I believe they need a hand–a slapping hand, not a helping one.

I don't know where they get their cheap pipes from coz they don't last. They are always broken and leaking. They must be making them themselves out of used plastic straws and cello tape.

Please let me give these guys a kick in a place that'll help them better understand the kind of pain and agony they put us through.

Many times in Kisumu we go for ages with dry taps. Then at the end of the month we get a huge water bill as though we had been doing some large-scale irrigation or something. It's insane.

There's this time we got a huge bill, more than triple what we normally paid, after a month of completely dry taps. So when we went to their office to file a complaint, they acknowledged the error and promised to make a correction.

That is yet to be done, 6 months down the line!

---

vii   *Electricity*

viii   *Water*

ix   *Kisumu Water and Sewer Company*

It almost makes you wonder what the man in charge of the place is doing when his workers (jokers is more apt) are juggling balls in the office rather than ensuring residents of Kisumu receive the services they are paying for.

I guess he's probably just given up on the face-painted, funny people working under him, and has now gotten used to them. From the way things are running, I guess most of these local governments and their utility providers have lots of jokers for employees. Coz Nairobi City Council doesn't seem to be operating much differently either.

They hardly do any of the things they are supposed to do. And the few times they actually perform their work, they erect a huge billboard to inform the world that they are the ones behind 'the noble deed'. A good example is the one I see every day on Langata Road: the city council put up some street lights along the highway together with a giant billboard to inform everyone who drives by that they are the ones who put up the lights.

It's almost like the lazy teacher who never turns up for his classes and for the few times that he does turn up, he makes a big deal of it so that everybody knows. This is crazy! I mean, isn't that what he is paid to do in the first place – come to class and teach? He's not doing the kids a favour by turning up for lessons and teaching them! Honestly, the only thing worth making such a fuss about would be a deed that is beyond the required, such as buying all the kids a pencil each, new uniforms or something else of value to their academic lives, but not turning up for class to do his job!

The City Council better use this as a lesson! It's high time it gave us a break and stopped thumping its hairy chest every time it does one of the many things it is supposed to do. The money wasted on these billboards could be put to much better use.

I see nobody's sitting allowance is permanently glued onto the seats of parliament! Is it almost 10 MPs[x] so far who've been sent packing?

Speak of a lack of job security!

But that's beside the point. Let's put the gossip aside and look at core issues.

First, the Constitution.

Mr. Prime Minister, I can't discuss issues, especially political ones, with anyone.

Why?

Not too many value my views. They consider them unacceptable, unreasonable and as a result, write me off as a mere idiot.

But then I wonder who the idiot really is when my divergent views turn out to hold some water. In the world of political opinion, you could say I'm the ugly duckling! I'm used to that negative publicity.

I end up losing many verbal battles of such nature coz of my inability to argue, especially with certain people. Once a discussion turns into an argument, I shut up and let it die down. (My upbringing shares a lot of blame in this. I was taught never to argue with "a certain calibre of people".)

Just so that you don't get the wrong impression of me, or even worse end up looking like one of these people I dare not argue with, allow me to inform you that I know the Constitution is a very vital document in every country, no exceptions. No government can function without it! And I appreciate that.

Virtually, the whole of nature is law bound. The ecosystem has laws such as gravity and floatation

---

x   *Members of Parliament*

to keep it all together. Without these laws, it'd be a disaster!

So laws are what make the universe what it is. And to me, the best part about these laws is that they are accurate, precise and concise. With absolutely no biases or favor, they act upon everything that comes into contact with them.

That's why when someone decides to jump off a tower, they fall to the ground. Gravity won't have any pity upon an ignorant mind. When someone decides to jump from the top of Times Towers, gravity won't be like, "Oh... poor John, you don't know what you are doing... I'll take you down slowly, this time only, so that you don't get hurt." It never happens like that! Whether you believe in it or not, you know about it or not, it won't treat you differently.

That's the best part about Mother Nature's laws, especially when you are caught on the right side. It goes unquestioned that laws are very important, and life cannot exist without them.

We'd have people looting their own houses, and *kangaroo courts* in every other place for settling scores, were it not for legal norms.

Even in homes, mums have to have rules that maintain some level of checks and balances on what their kids eat. Otherwise kids would be dying of cholesterol and heart disease by age six.

So this law issue is a paramount part of virtually all life on this planet. This is a fact that I know and greatly appreciate. Therefore, my stand on issues of the Constitution is not baseless.

My ugly-duckling view on this new Constitution right from the onset was not whether or not it should be voted in favour of or against. I wasn't eating from the plate of cheap politics of either the YES or NO teams. Neither was I partaking of the terribly confused words of the stanceless 'watermelon' figure. Proudly, I'll admit to eating off my own plate on this one.

The idea of so much time and resources being pumped into the process of recreating the Constitution at a time when more pressing issues were there to deal with didn't go down well with me.

It's easy for any informed individual to see that the country hasn't had the best of times since independence. Way too many things have gone wrong with no apparent action taken. All this happened under the rule of the old Constitution, true. But who or what is to receive the bulk of the blame? Is it the old Constitution?

Occasional massacres here and there have painted the country red. But little action has ever been taken. So who is to blame? Is it the old Constitution?

Or should we make reference to the more recent rise in insecurity and what's termed as 'extra-judicial killings', corruption, exploitation of citizens and corruption? Did I mention corruption?

My views may be very divergent, so I'm told. But for the open-minded, there is method in my madness. Allow me to explain!

When a bank is being robbed, what's the main concern of its managers and directors?

If the general security had been compromised earlier, now is not the time to fire the guard and look for a replacement.

If the floors were made of too slippery a tile, now would not be the best of times to try sorting that out.

If the sewer system were blocked and in urgent need of repair, the loo issue would have to take a back seat and wait.

If the customer service were on a down swing, this is not the time for a board meeting to discuss customer relations.

Even big issues such as the tea not being thick enough are forced to wait in line. It's not the best of times for the branch manager to summon the tea lady into his office and say "would you use a bit more milk in the tea? It's a little thin."

You see, all these are problems: the loo, the lousy guard, the thin tea and so on. The main issue on the table right now is the robbery!

Everything else can sit and wait, including pressing issues like the thin tea.

A new Constitution in a country with starving people, rising insecurity, too many idle youth, and deforestation that's run out of control, just doesn't top the list for me.

Of course there were those sections of the document that were in urgent need of amending. Those are the ones that required to be sorted out quickly, not the whole thing. Stuff like: regulations on the mental status of those who vie for seats of power, a reasonable minimum wage rate, a ban on holiday tuition in schools and so on. You know, just the stuff that directly afflict the lives of the masses as at now. The rest can get in line and wait for their turn. We must move systematically, prioritizing the most important stuff.

But now that we have gone ahead and created a new Constitution, I must say I'm relieved it went through, given all the resources that were pumped into the process. It would have been such a waste for it to suffer a similar fate as the other one in 2005.

I hope it will be able to deliver all that we've been made to expect of it. It seems to have some measures that are quite practical and should go a long way in helping us move forward.

You know most people fail to understand that the cause of most problems we have been going through as a nation aren't legal but ethical. Issues such as corruption do not exist because of an ill-defined

Constitution, but rather flaunting of ethical rules.

So in order to sort them out, we need to go back to our social standards and rectify them.

Sir, you are one of them, unfortunately. But I must ask, "What's wrong with politicians?"

I know in politics there must be at least two differing sides. If there were only one side, there wouldn't be politics, would there be? So there must always be at least two opposing sides.

~~But still, how does a normal thinking man (key words 'normal' and 'thinking') take part in making an important document such as the Constitution then vow to vote against it?~~

Forget I asked that! Let me cross it out! This is not an appropriate question... my bad! I know very well that many of these people don't even understand simple stuff like the water cycle, so how can I expect any better from them when it comes to complex stuff like the *katiba*[xi] ? That'd be like expecting both milk and eggs from a rooster. (The more urgent the need for that 'mental requirement' stuff I was talking about earlier.)

I acknowledge the fact that some of these guys take these imprudent stands not by choice but because their masters say so. I'd like to imagine that they are just but a small proportion of our MPs.

Please assure me that that is the case, coz it'd mean the people calling the shots (the real masters who sit on the thrones of power behind the scenes) are not plotting the best for us or they are losing it altogether.

---

xi   *Constitution*

_____

Can I ask you a personal question?

I'm not sure whether it's personal or not, but it's a question! And I'm gonna ask it!

If you were to describe yourself in one word, what would you say? (That's a personal question, isn't it?)

I'm asking this coz you fascinate me, Sir! This may sound silly, but allow me to say it all the same.

Have you watched the movie *Ice Age 3*? If you haven't, ask your 6 year-old granddaughter about it. But if you have, then you know my man Buck. I just love the part where he's narrating a story about his past then he's like "I died, but I lived!"

(I hate being compared to others. It drives me insane. But allow me to do it to you, just this once.)

This may also not sound too good, but that's just coz of my limited knowledge in language. But trust me, I'm going to try putting it in the best way I know.

You are like Buck in a way. You can raise the political temperature one day and take it back to sub-zero the next morning! You can die politically over and over and resurrect before the nation begins to mourn.

How you pull it off, I have no idea! It's like you have 9 lives, if not 99, a lot like a feral cat that has proven its immortality in the bush!

And you know the strangest thing about it? I don't care how you do it. I doubt if anyone really does. Most of us just marvel at the fact that you can do it.

You have managed to set yourself apart as more than a mere politician, and shown yourself worthy of being called a true leader. One who takes the front seat even when all hell breaks loose and actually makes things happen.

A few of the other dudes you have for colleagues actually watch your moves and see what you are doing. The bulk of them pay no attention and are caught unawares by the happenings. And instead of picking up from the mood around them, they are left asking 'What happened?' after everything has played out. Pretty cool! I must say!

I admire the way the slow-heads on the block are left with no option but to merely react to what's already occurred, like loser celebrities trying out a hopeless publicity stunt. They never act, they just sit there waiting for something to occur for them to react to it.

They look like silly runny nose kids who've just been punk'd. And to my shock, this same trick can be pulled off over and over again. They don't learn or what? It's like the person who hits his small toe on the bed every morning as he gets up and swears to do something about it only to repeat it the next morning.

Sounds silly, doesn't it?

Do you happen to have some principles and strategies that you play the game with? You know; a formula book of some sort.

I don't know how it works in politics. But in the business world, those successful investors in the stock markets, for example, owe a bulk of their good fortune to proper working strategies. They all have set principles, a bit like a personal constitution, that govern what they do as the market forces change. Every buying and selling decision is made as per the book.

So do you have stuff of that sort in politics? I'd like to imagine so. What's yours? Or you operate spontaneously, making up rules as you go along? That's what Buck does by the way.

Unfortunately, I don't live too much in the past. So I'm a bit rusty on my history. But the little I can clearly remember is that all great leaders since time immemorial have had a great team of advisors helping them make decisions and strategies.

You have this too, don't you? Is there some sort of regulation as to how many they can be, their social status, and so on?

How exactly do you build such a team? There is the common advice and warnings that one gets from friends and family over the phone, at the dinner table and at social gatherings. But when you have an entire country on your shoulders, you are going to need more than that. You'll need a team, a strong and well enlightened one, too. Which I'm sure you have, I can tell from some of the good moves you make.

So how exactly did you assemble it? More so when you were still establishing yourself and you didn't have all the vital connections.

In case you already addressed this subject in your book, please bear with me and just repeat it this once. Dad bought that book years ago (when it came out), but him and I are yet to pick it up and read it. We are working on that though, but don't get your hopes up. Being the typical Kenyan book-buyer, Dad just bought it and has been keeping it like a souvenir. I doubt if he ever turned even a page in it.

Personally, I doubt if I'll ever come around to read it. I'm a poor reader of such literature. I find it boring and hard to follow. Honestly, if it was a magazine on cars or something, I'd have read it cover to cover, cut out pictures from it and stuck them in my room long ago. Unfortunately, it's not! I may very possibly never read it. But I'm pretty sure it's a great book! For it to have attracted such attention as it did when it came out, it must be a good read. I still find myself laughing whenever I remember hearing politicians dismiss it without even reading it, a funny place we live in here, isn't it?

Sometime mid-last year a friend of mine was sent back home from school. Her account of what happened was that the form fours' dorm went up in flames one afternoon while they were in class doing a paper.

When they finally finished and walked out, they found the vast part of their belongings had been turned to ashes. Being its occupants, they were treated as the main suspects and sent home with the few possessions they still had left. Some of them went back home almost empty-handed coz all their stuff was turned to debris.

After a week or so, they were called back to know their fate. Everyone was to come back with a parent or guardian.

All the evidence, according to her, pointed to a form one girl who hated the institution very badly. The poor girl had tried to bail out using all the excuses her little head could think of with no success. Her mum would hear none of it. She'd even got kicked out of her classmates' dorm and was exiled in the fourth formers'. So in desperation, she resorted to petty crime – arson! This sure worked, her mother bent to it easily. She swiftly pulled her out of the place before being convicted of the crime.

With the perpetrator out of the picture, someone still had to pick up all the bills. There was no way the school was going to incur the whole loss.

As expected, the rest of the dorm's occupants were divided into groups and assigned roles in the drama. There were the masterminds, the inciters, the arsonists themselves and the chief inciters. Those who were absent from school at the time of the incident weren't left out either! They were assigned the role of coordinators working from outside.

Pretty cool, huh? Even the CIA doesn't investigate that well! I must say their teachers sure make good detectives. It must be difficult getting away with big crimes such as talking in class or skipping preps in such a place. You'd need to have the mind of those Prison Break dudes, wouldn't you?

Wow! It's like a movie!

These various groups were fined differently depending on how big a role they 'played' in the school's account of what transpired. Some paid 10 grand and others as much as 40. A great *harambee*[xii] that was for the school!

The culprit left the school scot-free so the innocent ones were the ones to pick up all the expenses. What utter senselessness this was.

It's insane! This is madness. Sadly, this absurdity is not peculiar to this institution. It seems to be the norm in many schools. Administrations appear to have gone insane. It's no wonder students go on rampage every now and then.

Let me not even go into the realities of the institution I called 'my high school', or we'll never end. It sucks big time!

I know of another administration that's got its head stuck between the knees. Can you guess what it is? I'll give you a clue – it's a lot bigger than the school's!

Before we get into that, tell me: what's the life expectancy in this corner of the earth? It's less than 100, isn't it?

---

xii *Fundraiser*

So now if I may ask, who decided that we should wait till 2030 before we start taking the nation's development seriously? Do you think he'll still be alive by then? Or he set it there because he knew we'd have a better chance of moving forward with him out of the way?

On a more serious note, do you really believe in this Vision 2030? If we honestly reason out, do you think it's a project that's ever going fly? Or it's just another act of blatant government mindlessness to waste more of our money.

I probably sound very pessimistic but if we just look at the facts on the table as they really are, it begs the question: 'Is anything being done in line with this goal?' Have we identified the key industries that we need to boost in order to achieve this? If so, then how exactly do we intend to boost them?

These are the basic questions we need to ask ourselves and find answers to. Probably the experts have worked this all out. But the average person isn't in the know of any of it! We – the commoners – must also understand this before anyone can dream of it ever going through.

It's like an architect drawing a house, then handing the picture over to a team of builders to put it together without any details of how they are to do so. They won't be able to build it. (This is your specialty, isn't it?).

Issues to do with the economy are my area of interest. So don't mind me if I get a bit emotional when laying out some of the obvious problems I've observed that seem to be going unattended. It scares me when people try to ignore a mammoth in the room. Are they waiting for someone to get trampled first before anything is done about it?

Back to Vision 2030. It's important for any

community to have a common goal which everyone identifies with and works towards. That's actually what makes up a community – a common objective.

A company, for example, will communicate its goals to all its stakeholders so that they are aware of what is happening and what is expected of them. That's the only way the goal can be achieved.

Up to this point (communicating the goal) you – the government – have done a good job at showing the nation a desired destination. Though many still feel detached from it, more so coz they live like domestic animals in leaking shelters in camps. Others just find it to be a mere national joke. More like a prank the government came up with on April fool's day that never died out. It's that laughable. Not that it's too big, but rather unreal.

I think this is contributed to a lot by the fact that people have not been given fine details of the role that they are to play in all this. We've seen the destination but lack a map to show us how to get there. That's why many of us don't believe it.

Before this thing can move any further, this information must be provided. It'd be pointless to pump any more resources into the project before this is carried out. The kids in school must know what role they are to play, same applies to the employed, the employers, the leaders – everyone.

In economics class we learnt that a government should have 4 main macroeconomic objectives:
1. Bridging the gap between the rich and the poor
2. Reducing unemployment
3. Maintaining a favorable balance of payments
4. Controlling inflation

The most interesting part in all this is that not all these objectives can be achieved simultaneously. There has to be a trade off. One must be sacrificed partially if the other is to thrive. That's fair enough.

A proper balance is what must therefore be struck.

Here is what I think about these objectives: I appreciate the fact that not everyone can rise to the same economic status. Depending on how you look at it, this could either be good or bad. However, I believe it's a good thing.

This is the basis of diversity in society. It's what ensures we have individuality, lifestyle and our very own identities. Therefore trying to bring everyone at par is both unrealistic and impossible. It would be a lot like trying to get everyone to wear same size leather jackets and tight pants – silly and impossible.

What should however be done is bridge the gap as much as economically possible, basically, lowering the numbers of those living below the poverty line.

How is this achieved?

Easy: increase the vibrancy of the economy by making the country business-friendly in all dimensions. In so doing, investors will be attracted to the region and more jobs will be created in turn.

Existing investors should also be treated in a manner that encourages them to continue doing business in the country and even invest more.

This idea of the rich creating situations in which the economy is so squeezed that they get richer while the poor get poorer should also be taken into consideration. I know it can't be completely stopped but it should at least be regulated in a way.

The issues of a favorable balance of payment and inflation rates also explain themselves pretty much.

For a country serious about its growth, the idea of run-away fuel prices should never arise. Sir, I can't believe the government did not have ways of controlling how crazy things could go at the pump! Who the hell decided to let oil prices be determined by market forces? Last I heard we were in a mixed economy, not a free one!

————————————————

I was chatting with a friend. She's really good fun to hang out with. That was sometime early last year (after the high school science congress). In the process something quite unusual occurred: the theme for the congress found root in our conversation: *science and technology for economic recovery.* I have no idea how that happened; we never talk about such academic stuff. But now that it happened, let me say of the theme that it was well thought and thorough.

Our school hosted the event at the district level. It was fun! My desk-mate and I had a presentation. The problem was we weren't able to fully prepare it as we had too short a notice. It was half cooked and some of the information on our charts differed with what was in our write up. It was a silly mistake, I know. The judge, who was holding our write up, kept stealing a glance at it and staring back at us with perplexity written all over his face as we made our presentation. I doubt if he understood any of it … it was pretty badly jumbled up. Due to that, we didn't manage to go very far into the competition. Otherwise it was pretty good.

But that's beside the point.

The focus lies on these two dudes who came up with an artificial womb. Brilliant idea, I must say. Some folks dismissed it, saying that it wasn't a new creation as such stuff already exists. But nonetheless, I had no beef with it. I only found it a little difficult, or should I say impossible, to make the connection between it and its role in our economic recovery.

When they were done presenting, I posed a question about this. What I gathered from an answer from one of them was something like: in a nation like Japan that does a lot of fishing, this will help increase their population and thus more fishing.

Don't bother rereading that. It's neither your eyes playing tricks on you, nor my grammatical error. It's just as you've read it – vague and badly jumbled up!

Oh, by the way, speaking about eyes, heard you had a bit of a problem a while back. How are you now? Hope they are better.

These guys' project has perplexed me very much. I've never really understood what they meant. I'm guessing they were reasoning that more people = more fishing = more fish.

Some punch in the face for economic recovery, if you ask me. I doubt if they understood the theme well, let alone at all.

Other dudes I know developed a school data base system for storing academic records. That was also great!

I asked this friend of mine about her views on whether or not it'd help in line with the theme. She believed it'd help for some various reasons she stated. One of them being that it'd help cut costs for the school by reducing its demand for paper... true.

But I had a problem. My problem was: our house is on fire, a lot like the girl's dorm at my pal's school. I doubt if we can blow out the fire with our mouths. It may work but we don't have that kind of time or that many mouths. We need a quicker remedy that'll have a bigger impact with the least effort. That means the neighbors should rush with buckets of water to help with the situation. And a fire truck too needs to be called in to work in conjunction with the neighbors' buckets.

I saw a brand new Mercedes Benz Actros fire truck in Kisumu, really flashy for a fire extinguisher. I just hope they have water to fill it up when the need arises. There've had bad history of turning up empty.

Likewise, our economy (house), is not at its best of times (is up in flames) and in urgent need of revival (extinguishing). Therefore we call in the neighbors' buckets (boost the sectors that are big employers – labor intensive) together with the Mercedes Actros fire truck (the capital intensive sectors).

I also imagined that, if say all schools in the country were to drastically cut their demand for paper by about 50%. What would happen to the paper manufacturers? Assuming that schools were one of their main customers, they'd be forced to lay off many workers if not to shut down.

With less demand for her meals, the lady who fed the workers will be in a fix. The traders who supply her with maize and beans won't be in any better a situation, will they?

If I'm not wrong, it's this domino effect that, once initiated and left on a free fall, knocks down many industries and scales inflation rates to alarming levels.

At times like this, when recovery is needed, I believe in preserving the life of every firm that's still alive, resurrecting dead ones and creating new ones where possible. The more vibrancy can be obtained from trade, the better for us.

Forget about cutting demand for locally produced paper. Rather, ways of making paper more affordable for schools should be considered, such as subsidizing its producers.

These are the kind of checks and balances that need to be set in place. We can't afford to leave our economy purely to the forces of demand and supply. That's why we don't have a free economy!

(In case you are wondering, I'm not ignorant of the growth predicted by the World Bank last year. Yes they said we are growing. But the fact is our economy is still down the tubes. Recovery is not too strong a word to describe what it needs.)

When talking about the economy, it's a taboo not to mention oil. This is the wonder commodity, the black gold, the only thing that money is second to in making the world go around.

I'm fascinated by the extent to which every economy on the face of the earth is entangled in this addiction for oil (especially the developed world). Squeeze the pipes to suppress supply and you'll either have presidents on their knees or war planes flying into your territory.

No wonder nations go to great lengths in the fight for dominance of this wonder commodity's supply.

An oasis has sprung up in the heart of the Middle Eastern desert as 'the world business centre'. Thanks to this black liquid.

It's mind boggling when you give some thought to the amount of wealth and power it generates.

When some idle mind decides to sing a song about "*kurudi ocha*"[xiii] coz life is becoming too expensive in Nairobi, I wonder if he knows what's to blame. I

---

xiii *Moving back to one's ancestral home*

wonder if he understands that the affordable prices he's accustomed to are drowning in a greasy shallow pool of oil.

The farmer incurs higher expenses in running his tractors and getting his produce to shops near you. So food prices are pushed up.

The shop also finds it more pinching to foot its electricity bills, fuel its delivery trucks, and make adjustments to employees' demand for pay raises. So what does it do? It pinches the consumer back – sets higher prices for just about everything.

People shed tears at the pump on their way to work. More so if they run a drunkard for a car and their name is Nathan instead of "National Oil" or Sheldon instead of "Shell", or Roy instead of PM, for that matter. The saddest bit is, for the bulk of us, all we can do about it is fight for a pay raise (but that's only if you have a job and are not on the verge of being laid off).

The driver of the *matatu* ahead of you in traffic is a bit more fortunate as he is capable of compensating himself by hiking prices as he pleases – just like the shop where you do your groceries. No one has a say! His wish is every commuter's command. His only hustle is the cops who want more from him to meet their growing expenses, too.

Question: you don't cry at the pumps, do you?

We (tax payers) have got you and your ranks covered, haven't we? That means you can literally drive up to the petrol station attendant and say "Hi! I'm not National Oil nor Shell, but I... I am powered by Kenyan taxes! Fill her up, boy!" Now that's the life.

Speaking of fuel, do you still run your Hummer? The H2 is a real guzzler. A review of it I went through a couple of years back said that at times it only does one mile to the gallon. That's one greedy American machine! No wonder it's so plump on the road, so rough and demanding of everyone's attention.

You'd have to either be unreasonable or desperate for publicity in order to buy one of them. It's a terrible thing for anyone living in the real world. But for reasons I can't quite place my fingers on, it's such a cool car. I think I'd buy one myself if I had a garage large enough to fit it.

And of course, the VW Passat!

Now that we are talking about cars, this is a great opportunity to bring it up. I can't possibly pass it up.

Uhuru finally got the nerve in him to crack the whip on the ministers and timidly say 'Return all your gas guzzlers and pick up Passats.'

I think that was a brilliant idea if your name is 'Uhuru the tax collector' instead of '*Mwananchi*[xiv] the tax payer'. This thing cost us a fortune! Some say this was just another feast by the minister and his people, a lot like the huge hotel that was sold earlier for a song.

(I'm shocked to see the guy who sold it still alive! Thought he said resigning would kill him. Oh, that's right. He didn't resign but got sacked! That explains it all.)

Anyway, is there any evidence that the cars they repossessed from the few ministers who obliged to the move were that big a guzzler as they claimed? You and I both know very well what the German automobile is all about.

The Italians, to start with, get high on excitement before sitting down to build a car. The result is pure madness that the rest of the world refers to as 'the super car'. They build raging bulls (the Lamborghini)

xiv   *Citizen*

and wild horses (the Ferrari) that are overpriced and not very practical in most of the real world. The one that tops my list though is their Pagani Zonda! A curious looking little thing, with enough horse power to relocate the whole of Nairobi a little further east if ever the City Council wanted it moved.

Logic seems to be of little priority to car manufactures in that part of the world.

Oh... not that they are the most illogical! Don't get the wrong impression. Americans rank pretty high too on the list with their greedy cars. I saw the Cadillac 16. In one word I'd describe it as – phat!

Okay, when 1000 horse power is stuffed under the hood of a super car, I don't have a problem with that. Why should I have a problem? It's a super car! If anything, I'd encourage them to add a few more.

But when Americans take the game too far and fit a mere 'luxury salon' with a V16 13.6 litre engine that generates 1000 horses, that's socially unacceptable in the global society. Last I heard of it, it was still a concept. I'm not sure if they ever got around to building it.

How can we forget them? Despite a rocky past few months, these guys seem to have learnt never to compromise on their build quality. I saw Mr. Toyoda (the president of Toyota car manufacturers) speak about this issue quite devotedly. (It's funny how his name rhymes with the company's, don't you think?)

Despite these challenges, they are still pretty much the brains of the motor industry. I really doubt if there's any other car maker with half as many models as the Japanese's Toyota car company. They've got a thousand and one! It's no wonder they are running out of names and calling their cars, Vista, Probox and that kind of stuff.

I mean, what would make someone give a car the

same name as a Windows operating system? And I don't care who used the name first, the point still remains that this is a name for a computer operating system.

Anyway, let them do their stuff. I totally respect the Landcruiser VX. What a proper 4-wheel drive. I've never been on a long ride in one. I am made to believe it's really comfortable though. How's yours on the road?

I may possibly be the only guy to admit liking the tiny Toyota Vitz a tiny bit. Everyone hates it so much that whenever I dare to speak well of it, people want to lynch me. But I like it a little. It's cute.

Anyway, I see we've accepted defeat in the motor industry just as in the many other industries we've failed to tap into. (If that's the case, why not lower taxation on them so that we can import more cars?)

Back to the people we should focus on – the Germans! They seem to have an appetite for 'inefficiency' and luxury. So they make the Benz and its breed.

Now that the Passat is from the same blood line, what makes the finance minister think it'll be any different? Let him not even start on the issue of it having less cc than the ones they took back. I've witnessed a BMW M3 (not built with efficiency in mind) give more miles to the gallon than a Toyota Prius (a hybrid). It's not about what car you run, but how you drive it.

Besides, weren't those Benzes diesel? That should greatly reduce their consumption, shouldn't it?

My! My! My! Didn't our money buy Uhuru a ride! Man that was an S class and a half! What I gathered from the media, if I'm not mistaken, is that the damn thing cost 60 million tax payer shillings. That should translate to about 12 brand new Hummer H3s that go for about 5 million.

I don't believe in poverty! It doesn't exist! The tax payer's got more than enough money to burn!

Word on the street is that he bought it from the government. I just wonder what he paid for it, given that the Benz has a "low resale value" and he was most likely the one selling it to himself. What do you think?

It was only you and Kibaki who were exempted for this move, right? Hang on tight to your Benz, dude. Don't let anyone snatch it from you.

Question: the cars that were repossessed, are they still around? Is their purchase still open to the public?

Si you sort me out with one of the new model E classes? I'd really love to have one.

Another question: what was that computer error crap this minister was on about that saw us lose lots of money? Can you recall that from a few years back?

What sort of comps does the government run? P1s or what? If it was genuinely a complication with the computers, tell the minister to talk to me and I'll hook him up with some new ones that won't bring him that kind of shame again.

We weren't done talking about how the cost of living goes up, were we?

Let's carry on. As I was saying, the guy who slashes lawns in the neighborhood will also hike his fee in an attempt to combat the war on prices at the shops. The guy who sells you water and just about every other trader will do the same.

At the end of the day, everything's price shall have gone up (inflation), life shall have become harder for you. But as for 'BP' and 'Shell', it'll be smiles all the way to the bank!

This is how the system works... pretty cool, I must say! It just depends on which end of the crisis you choose to be or are forced to be on. You can either be on one end with 'Shell' or on the other end with the common man (the one who's milked).

Trouble is, the majority of Kenyans don't fall in Mr. Shell's lot. They are the ones being milked and choked to death by the system!

The government's got to have this stuff in place that I was talking about earlier (the protective checks and balances). Coz of the way things seem to be operating on a 'free fall' basis is alarming!

Something must be done quickly to save the situation; more importantly, to save the common man!

I sat my final high school exam (IGCSE) sometime mid-last year. I don't know if I was fully prepared for them, but I did well enough. I'm not complaining.

Coz our time was so limited, we had holiday classes for two weeks over the 2009 December break, in an attempt to cover some of the remaining bits. It wasn't too thrilling a time. More so coz we had to go to school in uniform when all our friends were home sleeping and fattening up.

But I'm not complaining. I'm not sure school is designed to be thrilling and enjoyable to the masses. What I do know is that it's not the most exciting of places for me. Especially during holidays!

For many of the guys in our class, it spelt boredom in capital letters: BOREDOM! It was hectic more so coz many teachers were the ones skipping lessons. And the English lessons... oh gosh! Did I tell you about them? I probably didn't... give me some time to think of how exactly to put it. It's not easy to say!

Thank goodness it was only for two weeks.

Anymore than that and the little that's left of my IQ would have been flushed down the loo!

If you remember, this was one of the pressing issues I mentioned that needed to be addressed in the old Constitution. Sam Ongeri tried banning it by word of mouth but no one took him seriously. Seems Kenyans don't take orders pertaining to their children's education from those who alleged to have vanished with money meant for the kids' schools.

By the way, my begging of you to sort this out is not with selfish intent. Why should I care? I'm done! Rather, it's my patriotic concern for the children of this nation who are at the mercy of this killer's jaws.

During the last week of our tuition, on my way back home, I met some kid in the *matatu* I boarded. Unfortunately, I forgot to inquire about his name.

Is that what really happened? Umm... I doubt that I forgot to ask him his name! (I hate the fact that I can't easily lie to you! It's bugging me.)

So here is the truth about what happened: I saw no need of knowing his name and therefore didn't bother to ask. Besides, from his face it was eminent that he had a silly name. Good thing I didn't ask. I'd have been too disgusted to talk to him.

Anyway, I forced a smile on my face then turned and asked him where he was from. To my surprise, he answered, "school"... like I couldn't tell he was from class given that he had a bag, books and pens, clothes on, and a few coins in his hands for his fare. What a nice kid he was.

He left me wondering what my response would have been had I been the one asked such a foolish question. I most probably would have been like, "space" or "the pub" or "your grandma's place"!. You know, the right answer for misplaced questions of this nature. (It's like when you've just arrived from a long journey then someone asks "You've arrived?" What the hell? Why's he asking you that question when he can see you standing there?)

This kid went on to tell me he was in class 4 and that their tuition stretched through all the classes – from nursery up to the top most class.

About this point, I looked around and saw old parental faces chewed up with school fee stresses all around. So I decided to open my window, shut my big mouth and stare at the entangled Kisumu traffic.

My mouth was itching! There was something in it that needed to be let out and the longer I kept it in, the more it irritated my teeth. (This must have been the main contributor to my tooth irritation that finally landed me in the dentist's slaughter house.)

Come to think of it, I'm glad I didn't give that little boy the advice I had. It may have cost me my teeth but sure saved my neck from the fee-paying parents in the vehicle. They would have stoned me to death using nothing but the coins they had in their hands.

I just felt for that little boy. Honestly, Mr PM, what's gotten into our schooling system? It's built up so much snot in the head that its brain seems to have drowned in it!

What's taught at levels below 1st grade? A B C D, a little counting and sleeping, right? So for what reason would holiday classes be needed? You mean to tell me that three entire months aren't enough to teach this?

Do go ahead and correct me if I've got this all wrong. But last I heard, this was all they did down there!

With all the extra classes, it's like they are taught to count to a billion instead of to 10 or 20. And the alphabet they learn goes up to 260, if not 1000.

What kind of people do you think are being brought up in all this confusion?

Something is amiss, Sir. We can't afford to sit back and watch all these lives self-destruct.

It's no wonder so many people are in school but they fail to understand why they are there in the first place. An equal number are also there without knowing what they'd like to do with themselves upon completion.

Question: the fisherman actually went back home? Still can't believe it! He was so into catching 'big fish, small fish and all fish' that he ended up getting tangled in his own net! What a back stabbing spirit the anti-corruption commission's got there!

You know how fishermen are generally known to lie about their catch? Do you think this one was any different? I only heard him talk about the huge fish he catches. But I never saw any!

I'll be careful not to say he was lying, coz I'm not sure about that. I don't follow up too closely on the news, so I probably missed hearing stuff about it.

He swore to never resign and left the nation with a stomach ache due to too much laughter when he was forced to swallow his words as he got pushed out of office. At least the government was polite enough to allow him to sit in office until month-end. Being the most paid person in Kenya (at the time), that month-end salary meant quite a lot, didn't it?

What does he do nowadays? Do you have any idea? He's been awfully quiet; pass my regards to him if you ever get to meet him. He's still my man.

His successor's use of big complex terminology seems to be bearing fruit in sending chills down the spine of corrupt individuals.

I've never understood why holders of public office in Kenya find it such an impossibility to resign when faced with allegations of malpractice or incompetence. Their vowing never to resign only serves to erode the memories of their good deeds in the minds of the people and make them look guiltier. Honestly, if I held such an office and came under fire, I'd quickly resign and let investigations be carried out when I still have some dignity to carry back home with me. So many people fail to do this and end up losing the heroic view that the people may have had of them. They'd rather sit there until they are pushed out and are left looking like nothing but just your average loser who wants to cling to power by force.

Clinging onto an office where nobody wants you can only be likened to sitting butt-naked on a time bomb. It's going to blow in a minute and it won't be much fun!

Allow me to also point out some hooliganism that I've noticed lately: whenever a politician or someone working in the political arena takes a stand that is unpopular with MPs, press conferences are held to push for the person to resign and leave office. Now, I'm sorry, but I have no a better way to ask this: what sort of foolishness is this MPs are trying to show us?

Someone can't lose their job for merely taking a stand on an issue that is different from yours! That's nonsense!

This leads us to another suggestion for the stuff that required urgent attention in the old Constitution: a restriction on the level of imprudence that leaders can display in public; like the way you are not allowed to swear on TV and on radio... that sort of stuff.

Speaking of Kimunya, how's his friend (the bull fighter) doing? Is he good?

He's definitely got the spirit of the real warrior folk sing about! Tell him he almost made it into my 2010 book of heroes. He missed out narrowly. But he's still well-placed in my heart. Tell him to write to me some time, I would like to hear from him. He's been awfully quiet.

———————————————

Sir, you may have noticed by now how dearly I hold issues that directly touch on my peers' lives. I hate seeing people getting wasted due to faults that could have easily been averted.

Though I must admit, I've not always had this concern. There was a time when I didn't really give a damn, to put it plainly. And that was because I didn't know how serious this issue really is and I was also a moron. My eyes finally opened when I locked horns with the weaknesses of the schooling system. I guess it's true you never really know one's challenges till you wear one's shoes.

So that you follow what I'm saying, let me give you a tip of my story.

In my academic walk, I've been through many schools, especially at primary level. My sisters and I are what may be termed as academic tourists. We kept moving a lot, and each time we did so, it meant a change of schools.

At first, it took a bit of getting used to. But eventually, I couldn't bear staying in one place for more than a year. The change of environment, making new friends, moving into a new house were so exciting for me.

At one point we had to home school for about half a year. This I hated! Not having a crew to play with wasn't fun. I'm sure glad it didn't last too long! I don't know what I would have done.

After doing my time for eight long years, I'd earned my bailout. It was finally time for high school.

Form 1: the horror for many! Not to brag, but mine went well, to say the least. I never got pushed around, harassed and stuff. Things went pretty good.

What must have also played a big role in this favorable turn of events was the fact that I was voted in as class president, and that office sort of came with some respect. (The election was transparent and went well so there was no need for stuff like power sharing.)

I hate to do this! I don't want to do it. But if I were to fail to do it at this particular point, I'd be a mere hypocrite. And that'd mean, I'd look rather foolish every time I dared to open my mouth or take my pen in hand in criticism of your government, and that's a place I'm not sure I want to go.

So let me just get this over and done with. The sooner it comes out, the better for me. But please keep this between just the two of us; the crowd doesn't have to know.

Here it goes: in high school after being voted in as the class prefect (or class president, as I like to call it), I developed a sort of strategy for running my government. (You will agree with me that every proper leader should have one, right? And now that I'm telling you mine, you'll also have to share yours with me.)

Mine was a three-step strategy:

1st – Build a loyal following from across the board (make friends with just about everybody)

2nd – Identify with your people by fighting for their rights

3rd – Build a good reputation wherever you may need it

I won't go into too many details. I'll just give you a glimpse of what they entailed.

Step 1

I'm not too social a person so you may be right in assuming I had an uphill task as far as mingling was concerned. But ironically, implementing this wasn't too difficult for me at the time. Let's just say I was highly motivated! The reward was worth it, and I wasn't going to let it pass me by.

My work was made a lot easier by the fact that my most vital territory was only my class. And a good number of folk there were people I'd known earlier.

What exactly did I have to do? I had to bring all those who showed some level of influence over various groups (the cartel builders) onto my side. Once they were in, their crew members were in, too.

Where did this leave the few who refused to budge?

In a dilemma! A big dilemma! The pain of their being in opposition soon became too great that they'd rather submit and live in peace.

Step 2

A leader with whom the people fail to feel connected isn't a leader but a mere office holder. If ever the people feel their leader doesn't share in their pain nor know what it's really like to walk in their shoes, that guy's OUT!

This is one of the simple principles that many MPs and other office holders fail to see. No one wants to be represented by a person with whom they are not from the same planet. An individual who doesn't know the challenges that you face in your day to day hustle for survival can't possibly be entrusted with the task of making decisions in your best interest.

Leaders who don't know this suck! And they do so big time!

Luckily, Kenyans are wizening up. Soon this breed

of incompetent leaders will be history in Kenyan politics; banished!

This is the key to power in many ways. I learnt how to use it to create a problem then step in, before things get out of hand, with a solution. Pretty cool stuff. Not a very noble thing, but it sure works!

So that makes me not the best of leaders? Big deal! But at least my folk don't suffer.

Step 3

Win the love and trust of those whose love and trust you need. And treat everything that may tarnish your reputation in anyway like a loaded gun!

For those who must hate you, let them be. They play a vital role in keeping your name on the peoples' lips. However, when in office you must ensure that your haters don't grow too numerous. Coz if your math goes wrong, and this happens, you're screwed!

So there you have it; my 3 steps to ensuring total dominion. They may not be the most transparent (many things are done in the background without the people's knowledge) nor the most fair, but they worked well for me at the time!

This probably means I don't have the best of histories as a leader... big deal! But at least no lives were sacrificed for my selfish interest.

I guess we are all greedy for power. All that varies is our degree of greed and how far we may go in pursuit of power.

Anyway, now that you know mine, tell me yours. How do you run this town?

In my primary school days, I never really had any issue with school. I worked hard in class, played with the other kids (whenever there was time), got into mischief and endured the repercussions. I had the proverbial big dream of passing well and making it to a good high school. After that, I dreamt of going to campus, studying law then doing whatever it is that people do after that.

"But *vwhy*?" as Grace (my kid sister) would ask.

It had the money (at least everyone said so). It had a promising future. And it's what pleased everyone to hear I wanted to do with myself.

It didn't take me forever to realize that I can't deal with 3 types of people:

1.   Ignorant people (students)
2.   Sick, (possibly) dying people (patients)
3.   Law breakers not willing to pay the penalty (lawyers' clients)

In other words, I can't do the work of a teacher, a doctor (especially a dentist) or a lawyer. So that law thing I was telling folks about... I had to give it a bit more thought.

My passion however, has been in merchandising for a while now. I think I can therefore be of more good to society if I were to find work in that line.

When the concern for my future finally started causing me sleepless nights, I began to look around and read a little more. I studied the life stories of leading entrepreneurs like Sir Richard Branson and the likes. I wanted to know all I could about how they managed to pull it off.

When I opened my eyes and stared around, I saw people like Bill Gates, Michael Dell, Li Ka-shing, Sheldon Adelson, Larry Ellison, Roman Abramovich, Mary Kay Ash and many others who are some of the richest people on earth.

(This brings us to the question: what's your net

worth? In Kenya, where do you think you'd rank, top 10, top 5? Come on, confide in me!)

I'd be dumb to start blubbering on about how successful these folk are. Their wealth speaks for itself! So I wondered what exactly they did different from the other billions of people walking the planet without nearly as much.

My increased studying was an attempt to learn what it was that determined those who make it in this life and those who don't.

Where did this take me back to?

"Work hard, get good grades and you'll find a good job," the age old saying we all listen to. Seems 'education' is the recipe for success on this planet!

Probably that's why grannies and gramps who missed out in their youthful days are hitting up the books again.

It may not be very appropriate for me to go into the details of our education system at this point. So let me leave it at that for now, but let me just point out that it has some big cracks that need to be filled before it all falls apart.

The earth is heating up! This global warming thing has finally begun to dawn upon us thanks to the unbelievably high temperatures witnessed in some 'cool' parts of the country.

For a long while, people have heard about it. But it just seemed to be something in a far off land, happening to far off people. A lot like the war in Iraq, people starving in North Eastern Kenya, and the unfortunate Haiti earthquake.

Allow me to cite this sad ordeal that I'm sure we are all far too familiar with. Not too long ago we exposed our lack of concern for others' welfare by going to the extreme of pouring out milk and feeding it to dogs, and letting maize rot in the *shamba*[xv] while our fellow human beings were starving not too far away.

We can get that cruel!

Many families gather around their TV at supper time to feast their eyes on the evening news as their mouths feast on the meal they prepared. Their eyes feast happily away on human suffering and death in other parts of the earth. It doesn't even affect our appetite in the slightest of ways. We've become so accustomed to it that it no longer bothers us.

As we wipe the table and throw away the leftovers and food that's sat in the fridge for too long, we hear the news reporter give the huge figure of those dying with hunger in some distant part of the country or the world. Their areas are so dry and hostile. And the situation is only getting worse.

Basically, watching the suffering of others doesn't touch us anymore. It's even become a source of entertainment! It seems so distant from us that we somehow believe we can't share the same fate.

That's why we don't care about the environment! That's why those living upstream a river can do all sorts of things without any regard for the lives downstream that also depend on the same river.

People can still cut down hundreds of trees, mindless of the environmental cost to those in other parts of the country.

Our eyes only begin to open when a month-long national power rationing, coz dams are drying up, makes us sit in darkness. Once we begin to hustle for drinking and cooking water in our neighborhoods and we feel the scorching heat on our backs, then we know this is serious!

This is the point at which global warming evolves

---

xv   *Farm*

from being a mere myth, from a far off land, to a reality in our lives. That's when we begin to see the need for taking care of our environment. It's a bit late, but all the same...

Sir, I've made an observation over the many years I've trodden the face of this earth. And that is that we as Kenyans are the type of people who show very little regard for things that don't concern us directly. The pain of someone with whom we have no relational ties doesn't hurt us a single bit.

The need for beefing up security in our neighborhoods, for example, only dawns upon us when our car shares the same fate with the neighbor's that had been nabbed a few weeks earlier.

We'll throw litter carelessly, until it builds up into a mountain at our doorstep and make it hard to leave for work in the morning, before the need for proper garbage disposal dawns on us.

The exploitation of *matatus* by police only bothers us when we own one or two and start to feel the pinch.

And this is not our fault. I think it's just part of being Kenyan. It's who we are. It's a bit like being pushy, outspoken, or sticking out in a crowd of 100 for all the wrong reasons. It's what distinguishes us as members of this great nation to which we belong – it's being proud to be Kenyan!

When the media finally found a profitable story from Mau and gave it the limelight, I was shocked to see and learn of what was happening there. I know we shared a boat with many on this.

If you ask me, the greed for money is not only the root of all evil but also the root of all foolishness. You tell me, what else would drive a man to grab a huge chunk of forest and work to no other end but turning it into a desert?

True, some of them don't understand really complex stuff like the water cycle and the basic facts about the importance of forests in the ecosystem. But it's their greed that's to receive the most blame as it's the root of it all.

~~Shouldn't the government come in at this point and intervene?~~

Another dumb question... just ignore it. In fact let me cross it out. Who doesn't know that these forest grabbers are the government?

Shouldn't the government come in at this point and intervene?

This is the second time I'm asking you a dumb question, isn't it? Sorry about that. To compensate, allow me to now ask a proper one: now that the poor squatters have been kicked out of Mau, have the more wealthy grabbers returned our forest (the little that's left of it) yet?

You must know this. You were the one in the forefront of all this. Weren't you the one who paid the political price in the fight for the forest? (I loved this move! So precise, so well thought through, so well executed, so politically rewarding. Those runny-nosed kids must still hate it to this day.)

The kids who were fighting the evictions were on nothing but a sinking raft. They should have seen the water rising and the thing going under. I mean, even I know well that any issue touching on environmental conservation is bound to receive international backing.

And you banked on that! It may have cost you the votes of the affected individuals and brought you a little hate. The reward: international hero status with a reputation of solid gold. Nice!

Those who were fighting the move now look like guilty forest grabbers fighting to hold on to their stolen property. What a place to be! In fact, their little *harambee* where they each contributed what was left of their kitchen change was an act of political suicide in my book. When people have looked at you and seen the wolf in you, you don't put on a wig of wool (organizing a small fund raiser) to try and cause a deception. Who the hell do you intend to deceive?

Their selfish intent and lack of the people's well-being at heart was all too evident. They all made fools of themselves.

And who's to blame?

You of cause! You framed the situation in such a way that anybody who wasn't on your side wouldn't look too good. But they couldn't join you! Their pride and political standings at the time wouldn't let them. So you left them with only one other option – stand aside and wear the cap of shame!

I'm digging your tact! Seems we calculate a bit in the same way. I don't think I'd mind a game with your advisory team. If you ever need to redo the political rule book of this country, you know where to find me.

As much as you've had many good moves, there are a few times I've seen you fumble unnecessarily. But I guess that's just part of being human. We all get it wrong at times. There's this one particular miscalculation of yours on which I beg to differ. I can't say I know all the dynamics with which your team planned it to work, so I stand to be corrected.

But from what I observed about how the *kazi kwa vijana*[xvi] initiative functioned, I'd say a lot more needs to be done. It just wasn't enough!

---

xvi   *Youth employment*

Get my point?

Out in the Western World, as I'm made to understand, job opportunities are a bit more plentiful than here. There is work for most of those willing to seek it (assuming there's no financial crisis and all is well). Their governments, as I hear, are trying as much as they can to encourage employers to recruit as many *vijana*[xvii] as they possibly can. That's all well and good.

That explains why a pal of mine (I won't mention her name) often exclaims "God bless America!" when KPLC shuts the lights for no apparent reason, and taps run dry, and just about everything seems to be falling apart.

It'd be insane of me to expect all the government goodies they have from you guys. I understand that there are some differences between their economy and ours, so we can't copy them entirely. That'd be stupid!

That'd make our government no different from the confused copycats who parade around in the name of 'representing the youth of today' but are merely trying to live the fantasized immoral lifestyle depicted by what they see on TV and movies. We can't expect you to stoop that low, too. As a matter of fact, we'd not want you to do so even if you were capable of it!

That's why I personally don't say "God bless America," when stuff isn't too good at this end.

However, I strongly believe you guys should do more to ensure that *vijana* can get decent employment and opportunities after all their effort in school. This idea of making the process of seeking employment a full time occupation isn't too brilliant.

I don't know about you. But I find it a bit embarrassing that our government can only think of

---

xvii   Youth

giving us fields to slash and trenches to dig.

That initiative needs to go back to the kitchen – assuming it still exists. Oh. And this time, kind of involve us too in formulating it. We'd really appreciate being given a chance to be a part of its creation. I hope that's not too much to ask. You'd be shocked at the stunning ideas some of us can come up with.

Got it!

I've finally figured out a way of putting what I had to say about our English classes over the 2009 December holiday.

Quite a teacher we had. Times Tower, his knowledge and ego are probably the only things taller than it in this part of the world.

As our class teacher, he ran a tight ship where everything was supposed to move at his pace. Everyone was at his beck and call. It's tough to put it in a few words. I doubt if all this explanation I'm giving really paints the full picture either.

He was always punctual to arrive for lessons but never seemed to understand that, like the other teachers, he was also meant to leave when the bell rang. Or maybe he was just arrogant and had no regard for the other teacher's lessons. I'm not really sure what the cause was, and none of us ever got brave enough to ask him. So till this day, we still speculate as to what the cause was.

This issue of his with time always makes me wonder what it'd be like to have him as a preacher. I imagine he'd be the type that preaches deep into lunch hour with no regard to the fact that the whole congregation is dead asleep and nobody's paying any attention. I doubt if anyone would be bold enough to walk out on one of his sermons either, lest he calls down fire to consume them.

Quite a man he is. I wonder what he'd do if he knew I was actually talking to you about him. He was one of your people in the last election. I don't know if that has changed. What I do know is he still holds you in high regard. He'd be overjoyed to have a cup of tea with you. So if you could kindly do me one favour and take up my offer to have a cup of tea and a chat with my English teacher. It'd mean a lot to me. As a matter of fact, all expenses are on me!

However, I must admit that before I got to understand him, he'd really get on my nerves from time to time. He's so difficult to get along with, so easy to hate and so hard to understand.

He used to make me sick! I hated his lessons.

But I decided to try and get to know him. I decided to look at the world from his perspective and get to see things as he sees them. Not too happy a view, I must admit! He's not too happy to be Kenyan. He doesn't seem to like very much the fact that all is possible in this wonderful land of ours. That people in this country can rob graveyards and fit a thousand souls into a 14-seater *matatu* doesn't seem to amuse him much.

He is the English teacher! Unique, interesting, unrealistic at times and surprisingly understanding of others! I've honestly never seen a character like him. He is so cool!

He now ranks highly in my little book of everyday heroes. I salute him.

Oh... when talking about him, I can't dare fail to mention how devoted he is to his work. When it comes to job dedication, he's definitely the yardstick. That is what I admire most about him. (That explains why he was always extending his lessons and eating well into the time for our break.)

I may not be the happiest person to be Kenyan. But then again, who is? My former English Teacher certainly isn't!

That, however, doesn't make me a mere whiny weasel! I'm still very proud to be Kenyan.

When something good happens I speak about it, celebrate and try to remember it for a short while. For example, when our athletes do well, as usual, I share in their joy, and walk in their pride. When the rugby boys do us proud as they usually do, I share in that too. More importantly, when a useless minister goes back home, I'm overjoyed by that, too.

So I may be clinging on tight to the rear end of the 3rd class cabin of the nation's train, but I still find a reason to smile once in a while when a cool breeze hits my face.

The breeze that puts a huge smile on my face is the work that's been done, and is still being done, on the Nairobi-Kisumu highway. It has sure lessened the nightmare of the trip, and should go a long way in boosting trade in the region.

Thumbs up to the government for that!

On a different note, I am shocked to see people still living in tents. Didn't the government initiate a program to relocate all IDPs[xviii] ? What happened?

I thought the post-election wounds were all healed by now and only scars were left. Seems I was wrong though, wasn't I? The wounds are still as fresh as though they were inflicted yesterday!

xviii *Internally Displaced Persons*

That a nation can be so deeply divided along tribal lines is hard to accept. We are so discriminatory it's unbelievable! The violence that sparked off during the last elections served to paint the real picture of the magnitude of this curse we live with. People who'd lived together for ages as brothers and sisters turned against each other and shed their blood... gosh!

When things began to cool down in Kisumu to the point that kids could now come out and play, the ones in our neighborhood developed a new game. I doubt if they had a name for it, like most of their other games. It was pretty simple. It entailed imitating the evil acts of lynching the 'enemy tribe', banging on gates, carrying leaves and holding demonstrations and so on. They didn't witness any live killings, but they absorbed enough to come up with such play.

That makes me wonder; just what did those kids who witnessed more live drama, more live murders, absorb? I wonder what that eight-year old kid who watched his neighbor knock down their door and slaughter mum and dad came out with.

I can just imagine the kind of hate and thirst for the neighbor's blood and that of his tribesmen this little boy is forced to live with day-to-day. He must be quivering with revenge and rage. Picking up a gun and spilling blood would be a piece of cake for him.

Sir, you must be well aware that there is a generation that's going to come from these young ones that'll rock the very foundations of this continent, a generation of unforgiving hearts, merciless killers. A generation of brutal and selfish individuals who've been brought up at the altar of hate!

Who is to blame?

Let's have a moment of silence for all the lives lost in the havoc.

Silence!

Silence!

Silence!

Silence!

May they rest in peace!

And for the fortunate who happened to make it out alive but are still trapped in camps, get them out now! These people are there because of you and the rest in government. They can't continue to live like animals. Get them out, Sir.

If funding is the problem, cancel the unnecessary government spending and sort them out!

It is bad habits like these – tribalism, corruption and selfishness – that we've adopted that are now choking us to death!

Most of the problems that we face are thanks to these bad habits. We don't need a new Constitution to make our problems go away; we need to kick these bad habits!

My English Teacher may very easily be one of the most frustrated persons to be a citizen of this beautiful country of ours. He really amused me one time in class when he remarked that 'Kenya is the only country on planet Earth where people rob graveyards'.

I need you to listen up here. In some western nations there's a culture of zero tolerance of tossing garbage. People don't walk on to the street and dispose of their kitchen waste, neither do they roll down windows and toss cans onto the road.

There may or may not be legal penalties for offenders. But the people adhere willingly coz that's the way they've been brought up.

It's a bit like wearing clothes. Today nobody walks naked in their sane mind in most parts of the world coz it's just unacceptable!

We certainly have the clothes issue here, too, but we don't seem to care much about where our litter goes. We don't seem to have patriotism and transparency planted in us either.

It's really sad!

So with or without a new Constitution, our problems will never go away for as long as we continue holding onto these vices. In fact that's the very reason a new Constitution wasn't a huge necessity.

A lot has happened to me these past two years. I've practically lived three lives: as a high school student in Kisumu, as an ex-high school student touring the nation as he waits for his results, and as a college student living in your constituency. I think I've already talked a bit about this earlier.

The last one is what I've found particularly exciting. And that's coz of all the many stuff it's enabled me to see so far. It's not been even six months yet and I've already met a man-child! Yes, a man-child, in my class to be precise. Don't ask me what that is if you don't understand.

I've also met a man who can drive. And I don't mean mucking around behind the wheels of an automatic used car from Japan. I mean, pushing an angry Japanese monster like he knows what he's doing. I hate to blow his horn, but he had me seriously looking for my seat belt when he took me for a run. Pretty cool!

So I've seen a lot lately, both the good and the bad. But I don't think I'd want to go into too many details right now. I think it's best I leave it at that for now, and look for a better time and place for such talk.

If by any chance you do listen to rap and hip-hop, then you probably know that snitching ain't cool. It's so not gangster, and therefore not so acceptable to the people who partake of in the doctrine of the rhymes in these songs.

As this is something more in tune with people of my age bracket, you would imagine that I too listen to such music in the name of entertainment, in which case you would be right. You would also imagine that I too have bought into this cheap ideology of turning a blind eye to evil happenings around me and hate whistle blowers. You would be wrong in a way.

Because as it turns out, the man who won my 2010 man-of-the-year award happens to be an international snitch who is facing charges of sexual harassment. His sitting on my high seat is not as a result of his charges of immorality, but his snitch profession. It may not be gangster to have a world class snitch for a hero, but this Australian 'crock-man' sure did the undoable for me. I'm telling you, 'Wikileaks' is the bomb! There are many ways of giving governments stomach aches but nothing works like 'wikileaking' their dirty little secrets.

I guess we need to be careful of what we utter of others in the privacy of our bedrooms for our walls have ears. Henceforth, I will be sure to keep my vile thoughts between my ears, far from my tongue and teeth, lest they get 'wikileaked'.

If anything has mercilessly tickled me, it'd have to be wikileaks.com! Its founder: my 2010 hero.

I know that lots of panic flows down the spine of people of your calibre whenever this name is mentioned. I know that there are many people spending sleepless nights, especially when they know they've been backbiting some 'big fish'.

I guess it's reaffirmed to us the importance of being careful with our words lest the walls and birds hear us and snitch!

Before curiosity kills me, allow me to ask: when the government met to discuss wikileaks (after it revealed the 'stumblingly-blocky" view some of your friends have of you and the president) were you trying to look for ways to get wikileaks to shut up or were you looking for what to do with your friends? I sure hope you weren't trying to shut up wikileaks coz that would have been the worst ever use of tax-payer shillings! Everyone knows that once something goes on-line it sparks and spreads like an unstoppable wild fire. It literally goes viral and there's nothing you can do about it; just hush and pray that it dies out soon.

You must be pretty upset to learn what your American friends think and say of you in private. I think I'd feel no different if I were in your shoes!

There's really no one you can trust. Everyone seems to stab you in the back when you aren't looking.

Probably the most sober thing I'd say the government has accomplished this year would be the *Alcohol Law*. I'd definitely give you guys a pat on the back for it, especially the guy who came up with it.

It's going to be a bit tricky to implement though. It hasn't even picked up yet and it's already facing so much opposition. I know many guys who used to drink responsibly will now go out and drink like there's no tomorrow in a show of defiance.

I was talking to someone, not too long back, who wasn't too pleased about this new law. I think he's either one of the casualties or a merchant of brew. He was not a tiny bit amused by it.

Usually, I'd do what my boy, Roy, does in such situations: shut off my mind and pay no attention to the dude's blubber! But this time I listened *kidogo*[xix], coz he was looking at it from an angle which I liked – an economic one. According to him, this new law would cripple lots of businesses and cripple the economy of the nation, true (sort of).

Despite his rather emotional tone, he didn't reach out to me enough to make me buy his idea. I'm still with the government on this. This law will do more good than harm. It totally has to go through.

A few bars may be forced to scale down, breweries may have to come up with new ways of doing business, and some guys will have to get used to being sober for longer hours. On the up side, more productivity could be realized from the people who earlier woke up to go spend their mornings in some pub instead of doing something productive. Fewer people will be spending their days lying on hospital beds thanks to alcohol-related illnesses. Fewer scars on the face of the wife who's a victim of domestic violence, fewer children staying out of school coz their fee was paid to some bar tender instead of the school cashier. Less crime too... the ups are unlimited!

Honestly, when you weigh the lost revenue for brewers and liquor traders against added advantages for the nation, it's a trade off that's worth it!

There's really no polite way to ask this. But I really need to ask it all the same, so bear with me and just hear me out: does the government always have to do something silly to accompany their every wise move?

Seriously, how else would you explain this: we were told that apart from the regulated sale and

xix   *A little*

consumption of liquor, there would also be a ban on advertising of liquor on TV.

What do we see?

Liquor is being passionately advertised at prime time! What the hell is going on?

Sir, I care strongly for the environment. More so coz of all the heavy blows of retribution Mother Nature has been throwing at us (me in particular) lately. Clearly, she is not happy. Not that I have a happy history with her (she's always been grumpy and personal with me) but this time it's different – it's gone too far!

A while back she would precisely time her rain to ensure I got drenched every time I stepped out of the house, or zoom down the already close sun of Kisumu to scorch me even more, and many other childish things just to confirm to me that she's watching.

Now, however, she's mad! Seriously! It's not a childish game with her anymore. It's vengeance. This thing of global warming is for real and something must be done before Mother Nature decides to make life unbearable for us all (starting with me). As one with experience, take it from me. She can do it, don't test her lest she loses her temper and turns cruel!

Right now you could call me an eco-mentalist or whatever else you want, but that name calling won't deter me from putting my point across concerning what's good for our environment.

We really need to do something. And quick, too!

I strongly believe in innovation in sorting this issue out. We need to find some food crops and trees that can thrive in the dry areas of Kenya that are hard hit by drought, famine and poverty. That's the only way of controlling the rate of deforestation, providing a source of livelihood for the seriously marginalized communities living in these areas and boosting the country's economy, too. It's an ingenious approach. Everybody wins.

Other stuff could also be considered, for example solar power could be tapped from these areas. You know, just putting that idle wasteland to proper economic use in a manner that controls the environmental degradation and adds value to the communities' lives. The possibilities are endless.

NEMA[xx] should stop focusing so much on the kind of speakers on PSVs, and look into sorting out the pollution on our streets, neighborhoods, rivers and so on. They should forget the *matatus'* sound systems for now, and focus more on what their passengers are throwing out the window. You see what I mean?

If there's someone seriously concerned about the environment and not ashamed to admit it no matter the cost, that would definitely be me! I just want ways of controlling this global warming thing to be seriously sought. That's not too much to ask, is it? I have a lot at stake here, and everyone else does so.

Speaking of the environment, I have a little something that I'd like to make known: I can't wait for Thika Road to be completed. Man, I tell you, as soon as that super highway is done, I'm going to unleash an immortal beast that will roar on it upon sunset! A beast that only comes out in the dead of night. A beast only talked of in hushed whispers.

To give you a better idea of what I'm on about, let me alert you that this beast won't be one of flesh and blood. It may look like, sound like, and even breath fire like a dragon, but it definitely won't poop, and therefore will not be a dragon. It won't be of flesh and blood, but rather of steel and carbon fibre. Lots and lots of carbon fibre.

Purely inspired by my imagination of the perfect combination of add-on performance parts, you can be rest assured this will be no tree hugger! It will be the sort of thing that ferments grape juice when it farts and satisfies the need for speed of even the most insane of petrol heads.

Clearly, it won't be a hybrid either. I won't lie to you about that. It will be one of those things that drive Mother Nature crazy, literally! It will be the sort of thing that leaves the city feeling one degree hotter every time it goes out for a run of terror. Which is why I want to do all that I can to counteract this effect.

This is the childishly irresponsible creation of my equally childish mind. I just pray that sanity and growing up don't catch up with me fast enough to derail me from actualizing it. So these Chinese guys better hurry and complete the road quickly.

Oh, by the way, because of all the counterfeit goods that have been trickling into the country from China, the vast majority of us (myself included) have been convinced that anything made in China is not very durable. That is making me a bit doubtful of the quality of roads they build. I can't help but constantly puzzle my mind "Is this super highway the kind that is going to start having super potholes in a super short time of its super existence?"

Strange as it may sound, something in the back of my mind has been trying hard to make me believe otherwise about the quality of this particular road. I have no idea why, but it's trying to convince me that because technically this road is not made in China as such, but in Kenya (despite the minor Chinese connection), I may not have anything to worry about.

In appreciation of the amount of effort this thing

has been putting into changing my mind, I've also been trying hard to buy the idea. But it still hasn't convinced me, as all I see them do is use red soil to fill up the places where the ground level needs to be raised. I've not seen a single boulder dropped in to fill any of these huge gaps – just red soil that looks like it was mined in some remote Kisii village.

I'm no professional in building roads, let alone anything, but my little high school physics makes me doubt how well the soil will hold up the enormous weight of the road and the vehicles that will use it. Oh, I've just remembered you are an engineer. Please tell me what you think about this. Will it hold?

Or should we just sit and wait to see what happens?

As it turns out, I'm not the only one in our family with an unexplainable love of 4- wheeled beasts. Allow me to introduce you to my three-year old cousin. I call him Master JB.

Because of his tiny age, only tiny things may come to mind whenever you think of him. Such tiny things as:

1. a love for breast milk
2. cartoons
3. a love of toy cars

About mum's milk, you would be wrong. Turns out the boy out grew that long before his first birthday. Yes, he stopped drinking of it before he was one!

And about cartoons, well, let's just say I'm doing better than him. Apparently I enjoy cartoons more than he does. Turns out they are too childish for him. That's right! They are too childish for him!

So the only thing you'd be partially right about would be cars. But don't be fooled, he's not into miniature toy cars and dolls as the only worth he has for them is snatching them from his toddler sister. When it comes to play, let's just say that he has the mind of a man whose belly and age correspond in size to his fat wallet. He may love cars but he seems to be more interested in the ones too big to be driven on the living room carpet. He likes the big things, the real deal!

You may probably not understand what that means, so I'll be modest enough to put it to you in a language you may understand – English. So here it goes. Better listen up good because I'm only going to say this once.

The sort of love that emanates between a man and his toys is truly one of a kind. If you happen to be Christian, then you'd probably only second it to that which God has for mankind. On the other hand, if you are a drunk, you may liken it to what you feel for either your booze or your booze joint, whichever is closer to your heart... you decide. The point is, this is a rare love, and it starts from before birth. And as a man grows up it never dies out, *only that the toys grow bigger, more sophisticated, and more expensive.*

For JB however, his toys haven't taken Mother Nature's curse of growth. As it turns out he already loves his toys big and powerful. The kiddie business of driving a toy 4-by-4 on the carpet doesn't work for him. He wants the real thing. Seriously, he wants the real 4-by-4. Lucky for him, he's been able to obtain the real 4-by-4 of his dream and not just some cheap plastic replica of it from China.

Which car is it?

I'll tell you it's certainly not the apparently confused BMW X6, nor some weakling (seemingly) from Korea. JB's car happens to be the ultimate of 4 wheel drive. It's that car that, since white men began coming for *safaris* in Africa, has been the backbone of every such journey. It's very manly in every tiny way, and makes no apologies for not catering for the amateur driver!

What else could it be if not the 1993 Landrover Defender TDi County? If you know anything about cars, you must be blushing at this point as you ask yourself if he can drive it, too. About the blushing, I'm unable to offer you much help. You are on your own there, pal. But about your doubts as to whether or not he can drive it, let me remind you that this Defender makes no room for amateur drivers (which JB happens to be by age). So, NO, he can't drive it as such, yet!

But that's not been a sour spot in their relationship. JB still loves the vehicle. He calls it the 'Landi' Mark my word, in this little boy's world this is 'THE LANDI' and not just a car! He's very categorical of that and it would be rather rude for you to compromise it. Which is why I've warned you, so don't get it wrong.

———————————————

To be honest with you, none of us (his parents included) really know when this love affair began. I mean, how many people would expect their three-year old to start falling in love? Isn't that an adolescent thing that comes with pimply faces and uncontrollable hormones? Clearly, we were not expectant of it.

We only came to discover this affair last December on our trip up-country. Two cars were intended to be used on the journey: the Landi and a Benz S-class. The kids were to ride in the overly done German car (as we believed it would be more comfortable) and the rest of the passengers (11 to be precise) together with the luggage (which included a TV) were to go in The Landi!

(Not to brag, but I've got to point out to you that our remote home is not as backward as you may think. We have electricity, which is why we carried a TV along together with all the privileges of civilization we thought we might need.)

As planned, when we set off, JB, his age mates together with their mums went in the S-class, not to forget the car's owner who happened to be driving it. The rest of the folk and the luggage had the privilege of going in the Landi.

Sadly for the German car's owner, JB got bored of his car before they were even out of town. (I'm betting he felt the same thing I felt when I drove the car, a lack of thrill and all that we love about motoring!). Being three, JB felt no obligation to suffer in silence and decided to make his plea known in the politest way he could think of – throwing tantrums. And as they've faithfully served kids for generations, this sure mode of communication got his message across.

They pulled over and let him ride in the belly of his soul mate, which he loved for reasons none of us can really explain but only go about making our speculations. The vehicle doesn't serve up a very comfy ride. It's so rugged, so basic and seems to have more in common to a tractor that was built in 1993 than a German car built in the same year. And that's before you consider the other beatings: 400,000 km on African roads have taken its toll on its already unfriendly build. That's roughly the distance from here to the moon. So technically, this car has been to the moon!

I honestly lack words to explain this phenomenon myself, so if you're sitting there with your lower jaw dropped on your lap, know you are not alone. All I can probably say is that THIS IS THE WORLD'S YOUNGEST PETROL HEAD!

It may be true that petrol heads are born and not made.

So we now have it: the Ocampo Six, Resident Evil, the Fantastic Six, the Six Makers of Doom or whatever else we may like to call them. It's about time, huh? I guess it's no smiles all the way to The Hague! Ha-ha!

You know there are lots of things you can do to someone as a show of hate and stuff, for example you can spit in their face, torch their houses, then loot the funds that should go towards resettling them and so on and so forth. A lot like what the IDPs have been put through all these years since 2007. There are however some unwritten laws that set the limits of how far one can go with this. These laws are essentially what draw the line between us humans and pigs and apes. Therefore, when MPs stand before us on national TV to call for a fund raiser for the six suspects, they have crossed the line. That is going too far. That's rubbing the already thin line between them and the game of the Maasai Mara

What a disgrace? With so many people still living in deplorable conditions in camps, these guys can still think to urge us to raise money for those suspected of being responsible for putting our brothers and sisters in camps? This would be a good time to pick a word from the middle of the fisherman's curse dictionary and throw it at these people. Unfortunately for me though, Dad never let me get a copy of this dictionary when I was younger so I lack the appropriate words. I tried to tell him it would come in handy one day (like now) but he refused completely.

Anyway, I wish all these guys a safe trip to The Hague and a fair trial. May JUSTICE prevail!

Then there is also another lot I'd like to talk about at this point: the bunch of old children in government posing as youth leaders.

Tell you what, I'm a youth and these guys NEVER HAVE AND NEVER WILL LEAD ME ANYWHERE! Not to the loo, not to the bus park, and certainly not to the ballot box!

They disgust me, Sir. I'm a youth and I have absolutely nothing in common with them, other than being two legged. Seriously, if I went to the polls and found only their names on the ballot paper, I'd chew it up and spit it out!

It is nothing personal, but they just spoil every good thing the youth of this great nation should stand for. From the way they've been talking lately, one would imagine that if voted into office they would immediately terminate things that benefit the elderly such as pensions and stuff.

These guys don't want anything good for this country. I just pray they don't delude unsuspecting Kenyans with their vile doctrine.

They may go really high up my nose, but they haven't yet gone the highest. Trust me, there is another lot that's holding the title. I don't want to go into the details of mentioning names and stuff, but I'll give you a hint: they are three backstabbers hurdling together.

Got the picture?

With the immense pace at which time seems to want to move, 2012 is just around the corner. And it's a year with lots of anticipation of endings of many things. Hollywood believers are waiting for the world to end. Political enthusiasts are waiting for the curtain to close on the 10th parliament and President Kibaki's term. Nairobi residents who are sick of sitting in traffic are also eagerly waiting for the jams to ease off thanks to completion of the major road works in progress.

I guess nearly all of us are all pretty much looking forward to something big in that year!

And on this band wagon of 2012 anticipation, I'm not left behind! I too am waiting for something big to happen. However, I'm a bit hesitant. My reason being that I fear things may turn out badly for this country if the juvenile bickering that's been going on lately doesn't end soon. I'm very disappointed that you'd be dragged into a war of words with other politicians. It is so unlike you.

Please sort this issue out before we go to the polls. I don't want to see my country go up in flames again!

If I were to tell you all that I have to say, you'd not have the time to read it all. So let me stop right here, Sir. The rest will have to wait for next time, won't it?

I guess I've asked for a lot of stuff from you. But if you were to only fulfill two, these would be my requests:

1. Sorting us youth out. Any help you render unto us will go a long way into building the nation.
2. Relocating the IDPs still living in tents. They can't stay there any longer.

If you can't carry out all the other requests, then give these two your best shot. That'd mean the world to me.

Got to run now.

Hit me back.

Truly yours

Justo.

www.ingramcontent.com/pod-product-compliance
Lightning Source LLC
Chambersburg PA
CBHW030853270326
41928CB00008B/1354